ALL THAT'S LEFT JACK HIRSCHMAN

Library of Congress Cataloging-in-Publication Data

Hirschman, Jack, 1933-
 All that's left / Jack Hirschman.
    p. cm. -- (San Francisco poet laureate series ; no. 4)
 ISBN 978-1-931404-08-2
 I. Title. II. Series.

 PS3558.I68A79 2008
 811'.54--dc22

                                        2007051000

ALL THAT'S LEFT

TABLE OF CONTENTS

INAUGURATION ADDRESS BY JACK HIRSCHMAN

APRIL 14, 2006, SAN FRANCISCO PUBLIC LIBRARY

I'm honored to have been chosen by the committee of my poet peers and then definitively by Mayor Gavin Newsom to serve for the next 18 months as the Poet Laureate of the City of San Francisco. That honor bestowed has been especially heartening to me since its announcement on January 11 of this year because, in the many congratulations I've received from San Franciscans in every walk of life, I've sensed your sense of a cultural victory, not simply by way of my being recognized but by way of your identification with many of the struggles I've been writing about here in the past 34 years.

Of course, this small triumph comes amid an air of anomaly and absurdity, even where a poetic laureateship is concerned. For we all are inescapably in a time of war, in which the human soul is devastated to degrees that are immeasurable, and somewhere in that devastation in each of us, there are heard the physical bleeding cries of brothers and sisters young and old alike—and I mean Afghanis and Iraqis as well as Americans—who our own barbaric and monstrous system of greed and our own Congress of murderous cowards have decided must continue to be sacrificed on the altar of profits and voids.

I've said that I believe that everyone is a poet and that one of the central reasons that I've fought as a revolutionary is to change not only the material conditions of mankind but, in so doing, to liberate that idea—that everyone is a poet—into human consciousness.

Why?

Because language is indeed the house of Being. And its most concentrated expression is poetry. And poetry is the truth of Being. And that truth, which I call the most powerful thing in human expression, is precisely so because it defies and deconstructs Power. Because its own power resides in its expression of the end of Power through the verbal and rhythmic adventure of listening not only to what calls from within, but to the inwardness of material things and beings outwardly in motion, which not only live anew in their being named but, in their newness, in their being re-begun (for the truth of Beginning is all that Being is), also reveal to the poet their innermost secrets so that he might show the way to the light of the heart in the dark times of chaos and extreme psychic estrangement.

What matters is that a child of six in one part of the city and a man of 65 in another part of the city, both of them sitting at desk or table, writing poems, are embodying the essence of beginning and equality in a way that reduces all talk about beginning and equality to an exercise in rhetoric. Each is writing a poem. In the act of feeling. Whatever the content of each one's poem, the two are equal in love, though they don't even know one another, and Power is overthrown.

A radiance therein is being suggested, and let it be a preamble to a brief resume of myself, including some poetry, so that you have an idea of who I am and what the grounds are for my standing before you.

To begin, then: I love the sounds of words. My earliest memory is of the combo of sounds, "india rubber ball," which I heard as "indiarubbaball" (one word) in a poem, "The Shadow" by Robert Louis Stevenson, which my mother read to me when I was three or four. This was the beginning of my life as a poet. Then, when I was 12, I wrote and sang my first poem, a song-poem, "The Bells of Freedom," at the block party organized by my father to celebrate the end of World War II. When I was 15 I fell in love with a girl my age who carried a bilingual New Directions edition of the lyrical works of Paul Eluard, a French poet. We read them together and later it was she who led me (hallelujah for girls, young and old) to what I realized later still was, if not a communist then certainly a progressive political meeting. I wanted to be a journalist like Hemingway writing Spanish Civil War articles, dreaming of growing up to write a novel like *For Whom the Bell Tolls*. I'd already in the 15th year of my life been working for a weekly newspaper in the Bronx. Whammo! My first brush with the law. The paper was a front for a large bookmaking operation. Two guys in the other room worked a switchboard connected to a larger Yonkers daily newspaper, which in turn was plugged into the Yonkers Raceway. Busted at 16 by the Kefauver Crime Commission, which had come to New York to clean up crime, I was spared prison time because a last-minute deal, probably a payoff, cancelled the hearing, but the newspaper was forced to close.

A couple of years later, I passed from Hemingway to Joyce, thought I was Stephen Dedalus, and studied Latin and Greek (the keys to what translation abilities I have).

Leaving Nellie and Shep, my mother and father, and my teen sister Cynthia, I spent the next 11 years in Indiana, New Hampshire, and Southern California as a teacher in universities, with my wife Ruth and our two children, David and Celia. By then—it had occurred even in my last year at CCNY in New York—Jack Kerouac had raised our eyes to the Road, Lawrence Ferlinghetti to a poetry painted by the voice, and, in 1956, Allen Ginsberg momentously enunciated the narco-imperialist nightmare. All wrote in new American idioms born in the depths of jazz and African American longing for a Civil Rights Movement (just emerging), along with a Free Speech Movement.

I was teaching but writing poetry as well and involved with the latest motions outside academic life, influenced by those idioms but still rather europhile in my taste and sensibility. With the Vietnam War, I did some things against the State with my students and was terminated at UCLA. I decided to turn my back on the corporation, that is, the academic institution, and I would never return to that life again.

In those 11 academic years, I had published my first book of poems, *A Correspondence of Americans*, had translated with Victor Erlich a book of the poems of the 20th century's first Street poet and later revolutionary, Vladimir Mayakovsky (I didn't know Russian then but sought to put Erlich's translations into the New American idiom), and I edited and translated, along with many others, most notably the late poet David Rattray, the City Lights *Artaud Anthology*. My own poems during those years do not simply reveal my involvement with history and Italy but are written using American poetic techniques, especially inspired by the important poet and author of the "Projective Verse" essay, Charles Olson, by new post-Webern musical ideas, and by an image of the Tree of

Life of kabbala, an archetype of paths of energy in Jewish mysticism that I'd been studying for a number of years.

After my finish with academic life, I went to live in Venice, California where for four years I simply wrote poems, translated, and also painted, and that has been what I have done with my life to this day, with the help of devoted and generous women—all of whom have also been exceptionally creative people—and brothers in and out of the arts who have sustained me in countless ways. During that period I wrote anti-war pieces under the cover of introducing obscene and pornographic European novels like those of Georges Bataille, Oscar Wilde, and Alexander Trocchi, among others, through a pirate publishing house, and broadcast and wrote anti-war pieces and poems for Pacifica Radio and the alternative press that had sprung up.

I also translated a book written in French by the Haitian poet René Depestre, *A Rainbow for the Christian West*. That book of poems, about the invasion of the voodoo pantheon into the southern part of the United States, transformed me into a Marxist as a poet.

There, 50 yards from the Pacific Ocean, on the western edge of the States, I also engaged in an extraordinary correspondence with the San Francisco-based poet, intellectual, and kabbalist-activist, David Meltzer. There too memories of my life in the Bronx welled up. One of the poems of that period that still perhaps speaks to the contemporary moment is "Ghetto." My voice at that time is still idiomatically penetrated by fellow poets Amiri Baraka and Allen Ginsberg, but the structure of the work, and its drive, are very much my own:

GHETTO

Men fight. With their fists in the balls of their mouths
in the silence between they bitch out their boys. At
the shabby corner store they cut each other to ribbons,
stand up skinny pricks against the damp mackinaw wall
of skyblue chalkstick death in Kingsbridge in Fordham down
at Hunt's Point in Pelham I pass through three and a half
room hands my profile still set against the black girders
and rattling trains, my dark books still scared of the shiv
and rumble of Jerome and Elder *mira mira* my face at Bath-
gate Freeman they are dropping sensations out of the *Daily
News* trucks I have attacked an eight-year-old boy in the
ruins of Starlight Park near the bones of the Coliseum
and the cheeseboxes with cut-out eyes open into the anger
of housedresses all inscribed in corduroy terror by a left
back with tongue slobbering somewhere in the upper reaches
of his gums on a blacksatin Friday night a cellardoor o-
pening to the sky import strictly from Harlem is muffed
on the cushions by a million pimples. And this my chassidic
teacher is where I go back to begin from. Na, share this
dead bowl of kaddish we go downtown:

       black island ghost blocks at dawn drubbed stumbling
hypnotic cold hungover and eerie,
       his pride sticking out of his sock her face kissing
Jerusalem's early suicide on East 33rd on Bleeker,
       my broken bottleneck for kill,
       my paperbag sherry,
       black dada nihilismus wizardry of the kissed ass,
       tomorrow's loot music,
       all the evil haberdashery of roach fingers crawling all

over the whites of their eyes,
        sewers lined with dynamite,
        vein streets junk bulletholes in the rock island arm suck-
ing animals at midnight,
        eat the heart of massa and throb Kong,
        beat hisself to death and die alive man the
                                        screaming
next door will you shut up for chrissakes,
        Bird is walking on the waters of piss,
        gutter hoarse and fogged with slush affections,
        The Trane is setting,
        she stink the summer armpit the winter burning cold
compassion,
        she tell me to my face gutter you go out and get a coat,
        she bang on my rib radiator wake up to the black sun,
        with tired shoes she springs.

        Who showed you the rot in the ring and smiled fear?
        Pointed to jail and bawled at the bars of your freedom?
        Put the blear and round of this world in your eyes
        so that only the shades and the shadows would do?
        Taught you the motherfuck? beat hell
        out of night so you finally could get some shuteye?
        Bum. Scuffle. Before and behind. While your mother
        was having a heartattack and your old man my foot
        went shellacking the sidewalk in search of an
        eight-ounce mitt he could call the pride of his son?

                Golem
                        me make you bitter
                sweet numbers and letters
                        dialed to a hundred no's

from the rotten heart
           beat you ate
—*conceited!*—
out of garbage cans and crumpled
teachings
out of the bratty insolences
of the old and young alike
out of hooey and dig the bam the
crack the jerkoff
under the yellow bulb inside
the tarnished mailbox and warped
green paint of the door always
slamming behind the elevators too
cramped or bowls with the retch of
the wretched
                          come
                                    to your teeming
shores to raise a John
           who be my just disciple
                 Golem
              assassinated Golem of
                          war Golem weary
                 Golem pitiful
                 Golem juice is all
run dry and goes on speed and goes
in drag
       Daddy Warbucks pileup
             Muscle hanging limp
          at the beginning and the end of all
                 Our Brag.

Early in 1973, in San Francisco by then, after some weeks on Leavenworth Street, I made North Beach my village and lived first in the now defunct New Riveria Hotel, and then with the artist Kristen Wetterhahn in a flat on Kearny Street. The true history of North Beach in those years of the '70s and into the '80s is not written in words but rather in the napkin portraits that Kristen drew— she can write a face better than anyone around—faces of people visiting from other neighborhoods and other countries to the cafés of North Beach in that time of war and lunacy. After three years writing and translating from Italian, Spanish, French, German, and Russian, one day early in 1977 I wrote my first poem in Russian, in the Caffé Trieste in North Beach, where I did most of my translating. It went like this:

YOU ARE NOT A SLAVE

ТБі нет раБ и я нет машина
И ето нет опиумнои сон, товарищ.

You are not a slave and I am not a machine
And this is not an opium dream, comrade.

It was a playful poem, but a serious one as well, for all my street-hearts who smoked shmoogadoo (my name for marijuana), and it was a precursor of my organizing days to come. To go beyond dope, call yourself a communist, and then ACT upon your words and struggle for collectivity, are not easy things to do in this society of sellers of fish, I mean this sel-fish, with its sel-finterests, society. With the Russian language (I wrote a poem a day in Russian for the next 11 years), as well as my own American language, I then fully entered a domain of international engagement (the other languages had already confirmed that, but Russian was the language—in my mind, at least—of Mayakovsky, Lenin, the Bolshevik Revolution).

Within the next three years, I'd become part of a cultural group preparing for the Sandinista Revolution in Nicaragua, working with Roberto Vargas, Alejandro Murguia, Jim Willems, and many other *compañeros* opposed to the Somoza regime, which fell in 1979. The next year I entered the Communist Labor Party, a small party in comparison with others but one which I found amenable not only because of its principled and thorough analyses of matters in this country and Mexico, but because the CLP was open to poetry. I wasn't the only poet among the cadres. The Chicano poet Luis Rodriguez was among us, as well the African American Michael Warr, the Japanese-American Kimiko Hahn, the Irish-American Frank Furey, and many others—all contributed to the cultural dimension of the CLP's program.

The CLP taught me compromise. Not the compromise that means "sell-out," not the Hollywood happy ending when everything else in the film insists upon an ending that isn't faked and contrived, but the compromise demolishing the capital P for Poet/ego and leading one, through the most beautiful coercion—a coercion of self-realization—to put one's deepest abilities at the service of the working-class struggle for liberation from the yoke of capitalism. I who had come from the quote lower middle-class unquote—like many writers and artists of my generation in New York City and elsewhere after World War II—found, in the leap of identity with the poor workers, Blacks, Latinos, the unemployed, the immigrants, where the energies of my poems' contents really came from. And it was then that I realized I was being called by another set of demands than the ones in which the poet writes for other poets, sees the avant-garde as a group of poets or artists. In a little poem of that time, there is a sense of where I am headed. The title, "XLEB," means "Bread" in Russian:

XLEB

From the top here
of Vesuvio's
I have just seen
a man with
spectacles
and a beard
come along
Adler's Alley
roughly
twenty-five years old
to the garbage bin and reach
in and lift
out a container
of pistachio
icecream
and lick it
with his fingers,
then reach in
for a piece of paper
and wipe his fingers
very delicately
and his mouth
very elegantly
and continue
on into the
mainstreet, what
can you
say to this
piece of bread?
Dostoyevsky?

During the next years of the '80s, a number of events came to matter very importantly. For one, I met Csaba Polony, an artist and publisher of *Left Curve* magazine, with whom I have worked to this day. Originally born in Hungary and raised in Ohio, Csaba has worked pretty much all of his adult life to produce an annual issue of a magazine also governed by strong principles, and he has fine instincts for publishing very socially and politically engaged articles and poetry. Ours has been a deep and rewarding fraternal relationship rooted in both Marxist and Heideggerian thought these many years.

Shortly thereafter, the death of my son David—a jazz announcer in Santa Cruz—at age 25 from lymphoma, devastated my life. Until then I'd believed that the most tragic event in American life had been the events of Jonestown (with the exception of 9/11 but, in part, even including 9/11, I still believe that)—tragic in the sense that the effects are the most profoundly immeasurable. So too are the effects of my beloved son's passing. Nothing simplifies more deeply than does Death.

With the coming to power of Ronald Reagan, the Left in this city began mobilizing against him. The Left-Write—spelled W r i t e—conference of poets, writers, and intellectuals convened, and out of it was developed, among other things, a collective of translators of revolutionary poems from all over the world, with American poets being translated into other languages, and the issues sent to 50 countries, to revolutionary cadres or writers' unions. There was no editorial board listed but among the most stalwart through those years were Carol Tarlen and R. V. Cottam, both now gone but never forgotten, working-class poets of great commitment, as were David Joseph, Francisco Alarcón, Dimitri Charalambous, Jorge Argueta, Bruno Gulli, Donna Kelso, and Gary Sea, to name but a few of the many who translated for *Compages* throughout the '80s.

During this period as well, the Haitian poet Boadiba and I founded and organized a Haitian cultural support group, the Jacques Roumain Cultural Brigade, named after the poet-novelist and co-founder of Haiti's first communist party. We worked in collaboration with Paul Laraque, who headed up the Association of Haitian Writers Abroad in New York. We published a poetry newsletter called *Boumba (Canoe)*, which included translations of Haitian poetry written both in French and in the native Creole. One of the Brigade's members, Rosemary Manno, translated a book of Laraque's marvelous poems, *Camourade*. Some of Jacques Roumain's work was translated by another member, Ronald F. Sauer. And the large anthology of poetry called *Open Gate*, translated from Haitian by Boadiba and myself, presented a wide range of some of the most interesting poets of perhaps the most devastated country in the Americas.

We organized events to shed light on the cruelties of the Baby Doc Duvalier dictatorship in Haiti. Those were days of many national liberation struggles, spurred on by the Sandinista victory in Nicaragua. Following a grouping in Mexico, Alejandro Murguia and Magaly Fernandez called for the formation of the Roque Dalton Cultural Brigade (La Brigada Cultural de Roque Dalton), named after perhaps the finest poet of El Salvador. This collective also included poets and intellectuals like Francisco Alarcón, Juan Felipe Herrera, Margarita Robles, Barbara Paschke, David Volpendesta, Tony Ryan, Wilfredo Castano, Walter Martinez, Tina Alvarez Robles, Cecilia Guidos, and a grand *compañero* musician, Jorge Molina. Apart from events, we published an anthology of Central American poetry, edited by Murguia and Paschke, and translated by Brigade members and other *compañeros*, entitled *Volcan*. Then we published *Tomorrow Triumphant*, the poems of the murdered Guatemalan poet Otto Rene Castillo. It was edited by Volpendesta and Fernandez and translated by Brigade members. The third book we published, Roque Dalton's *Poemas Clandestinos (Clandestine Poems)*, I had actually translated three years before the Brigade was formed, but we collectivized its presentation: Barbara Paschke thoroughly edited my versions, and our *querida compañera* Margaret Randall wrote the introduction.

My life in this period had greatly changed. I was living with another woman, the poet Sarah Menefee, whose sensibility was of, toward, and for the working class, through and through, and whose poetry, of the most vulnerable beings on the street, is radiant with compassion's luminosity.

Our work with the CLP deepened, ignited by its collective depth and by the brilliant insights of comrades in all walks of life, and especially those of an African American in the CLP, a revolutionary of the highest order of dialectical understanding, Nelson Peery, the author of *Black Fire*. All of us in the CLP already were aware in the early and mid-'80s that homelessness was becoming pervasive. The CLP—and I say this with great pride—was the only party that engaged that problem from the get-go, understanding that robotization and electronic production in the hands of the capitalists would be decimating the workers in the future, though technology itself can actually house, feed, and clothe everyone on earth for the first time in human history.

It's one thing to fight for the national liberation of peoples of other countries. But it's here that the belly of the beast is fully bloated. We threw ourselves into the struggle; Sarah, along with homeless activists and homeless people, organized the first Union of the

Homeless in this city, actually sparking a strike of a downtown shelter. Other actions, with Food Not Bombs and Homes Not Jails, were rousing the people to become aware of the poverty the ruling class was throwing so many into. Activists like Chance Martin, of the Coalition on Homelessness, and me like to recall those wild days of marches and confrontations with City Hall, the jail cells we were housed in on different occasions after actions. And who can forget Keith McHenry, that superb provocateur who initiated Food Not Bombs in San Francisco and was always in the faces of the cops, or Ted Gullickson, who, at the start of Homes Not Jails, was like a whisper and then developed into a torrid spokesman for tenants' rights, and still carries on in that fighting capacity? And there are so many more, men and women both, who hold the righteous torch of social struggle high. Yes, the Beat poets went on, but it was the Street poets who united with common causes and played active and activist roles, who represented the Street at its most conscious and, as far as I am concerned, the most exciting poetry in San Francisco.

During those years and into the '90s and even the Millennium, I also translated a number of books of women poets, from Russian (Natasha Belyaeva), from Greek (Katerina Gogou), from Spanish (Luisa Pasamanik and Ambar Past), from German (Sarah Kirsch), from Yiddish (Malka Heifetz-Tussman), and from Italian (Anna Lombardo and Lucia Lucchesino).

With the voluntary—that is, collectively agreed-upon—dissolution of the Communist Labor Party for the simple reason that technology was forcing the creation of a new class of poor people, the old communist forms of structure could not be sustained. To get into the trenches with the poorest, and those threatened with homelessness though they worked, we needed to work toward the creation of a party of those 37 million folks who live in the direst kind of need in this country, and the 40 more million who live below the poverty level, just holding on. Four years after the CLP dissolution, the League of Revolutionaries for a New America—a non-party grouping of guerrillas of education about the New Class and its formation through intense robotization, job loss, and runamok capitalist consolidation—came into existence. Naturally, as the oldest consistent newsboy in San Francisco, I joined on. You know I take the common sense of the *People's Tribune* to be very necessary in an age of media lies and misinformation.

But while ever available to present my poems on issues of homelessness, immigrant rights, and tenant issues, I'd also begun to travel to Europe because two of my books, published by Curbstone Press, had been translated into Italian by Bruno Gulli. As someone always close to European society, in sensibility and through my many translations, I began—what has continued for a dozen years— to make annual reading tours of Italy and France (where my books also have been translated, by Gilles B. Vachon), and these trips have included visits to Slovenia, Bosnia, Germany, Sweden, and England.

These are not simply trips abroad. I meet or learn of many poets in other lands and have translated and published their works in this country, at times for the first time—wonderful poets like Ferruccio Brugnaro, Alberto Masala, Sante Notarnicola, Ugo Pierri, Sandro Sardella, Pier Paolo Pasolini, Igor Costanzo, Rocco Scotellaro, among others in Italy, and Cletus Nelson Nwadike, a Nigerian who writes in Swedish, and Ismael Ait Djafer, an Algerian who wrote in French. I believe that translation is undoubtedly one of the most important human dispensations toward making the world a more consciously harmonious ground for brother-and sisterhood.

In the last-named country, at an international festival of poets, the Swedish-born poet and artist Agneta Falk and I began a relationship that has continued to this day. Aggie writes a vividly social poetry herself, with a confidence fearless enough to confront the most negating forces, and, as a painter, writes poems into her canvasses as well. She has helped to intensify what has been the major poetic drive in my life for a number of years. That is, back in 1972, just as I was leaving Los Angeles, I'd begun a series of orchestrated, longer poems called *Arcanes*. In short, I'd found the compositional voice for what has developed through the years into my masterwork, a mirror of the generation from the 1970s to the present day, in the form of works whose structural meaning I hope will provide rhythmic and philosophical strength for the soul in the chaos which is the condition of our time.

My shorter poems, some of which you have heard, have been recently collected in the City Lights *Front Lines* edition of 50 years of my work, as well as in two chapbooks published by Sore Dove Press. Three bilingual editions of 23 *Arcanes* have been published by Multimedia Edizioni, 16 of them translated by Raffaella Marzano, three by Anna Lombardo, and four by Mariella Setzu. Now a massive edition of all 126 *Arcanes* has been published only in American in Italy, with introductions by Sergio Iagulli and David Meltzer, and a copious bibliography of all my works compiled by Matt Gonzalez, whom many of you know as, among other things, a great friend of poets and artists of this city, and who made possible the most exciting and poetic political campaign in my lifetime and the lifetime of many other San Franciscans.

Before I close this address with a reading of one of the *Arcanes*, the one I publicly read two weeks ago at the large anti-war rally, and because your patience with this biographical tour of mine must have included a bit of impatience for me to get to what I'm going to do as the Poet Laureate, let me say this:

Apart from my participation in the Lit-Quake events on Valencia Street, which is part of the mandate for the Laureate, and my continuing writing for and participation in events involving the issues of our day—especially as they touch upon the material as well as the cultural needs of the people of San Francisco—I along with others will organize a giant three-day festival to occur in the early months of next year. This festival will be international in scope. Poets from other countries will be invited to join in readings with the best of San Francisco's poets. By which I mean the most passionately and socially engaged voices. My own experience in the last few years has shown me that Youth Speaks contains some of the most exciting poets in the city, and so they will be represented. As will the best of hip-hop, whose form has sparked the greatest migration of poetry to other countries since the Beat years. And the best of the Street poets of the city, and the poets of passionate deconstruction will be invited as well.

I will also be working with Marcia Schneider and the staff here at the San Francisco Library to continue the excellent inclusive work of the preceding Poet Laureate, devorah major, whose democratization of poetic presences from everywhere in the city I count as truly stunning. Furthermore, I will call upon the Supes of each of the 11 districts to put culture on their agenda by tapping their own districts and organizing, with my help, a monthly reading of poets living in said districts, each month a different district. And these readings should include original languages and translations from the wide spectrum of languages in San Francisco—Chinese, Vietnamese, Arabic, Russian, Greek, Amharik, Yiddish, Hindi, Haitian, Japanese—as well, of course, as Italian, French, Spanish, and German—for there are poets writing in other languages all over this town.

Finally, and uniting with the suggestion of Gardner Haskell of the San Francisco Library, I will do all that is necessary to bring about the creation of Poet's House in San Francisco. This will be a space for events, for a library, and will also contain within it—and finally achieve a home for—the poet Kush's Cloud House, one of the largest audiovisual collections of poets in the United States. Over more than 30 years, Kush has taped not only the poets of this city but visiting poets from other places in this country and visiting poets from other countries on this planet. It's about time his work was given the honors it deserves, and the creation of Poet's House—which will serve the whole city's cultural communities—will do just that.

There's a poet, as we know, behind every espresso cup here in San Francisco. Many write in anonymity, even clandestinely, yet everywhere the human poetic soul knows how to deconstruct Power. If I said the most important poet in the Americas for the past dozen years is a man named Rafael Guillén, most present here might not even know who I was talking about. But Guillén, a revolutionary poet and intellectual, at a certain point in his life found his cause among the indigenous poor, whom he has not only helped to organize but from whom he has received some of his most profound poetic inspiration. He has embodied, as a comrade has said of him, the idea of "the word as a weapon deployed in the shadow of the gun," and led a major defiance against the evils of NAFTA and other corporate dislocations, using the poetic word as the finest example of manifest testament as well as political strategy. For that reason, I hold Subcomandante Marcos, his public name, lately permutated into Delegado Zero, in the highest regard and hope in the coming period that voices for the New Class of poor will emerge here in San Francisco with even greater fervor and hope, nourished by his example and that of the Mayan people of Chiapas. Let's open ourselves within to the truth of the real needs of our people and let the winds of deep change blow through us, projected forward by the words and the voices of the poets who can make tomorrow die to become today.

The word "Quntzeros" in the closing poem's title is a medieval Hebrew word meaning a tract, or a pamphlet:

THE QUNTZEROS ARCANE

To throw a monkey-wrench
into the total
mobilization of the Empire machine,

for those "under a sun with
its throat cut since birth,"
a "sun born in chains
that only shines at night,"
where dogs are eating
dead bodies in the streets,
and roots are captivity,
and the simplest bread groans
before it even enters a mouth,
where revenge goes hand in hand
with desolation with the School of Suicide,

enter this thickly carpeted chamber,
unbuckle your belt from around
your religious waist;

and with those who want to kill
the killers, and those who want
to kill those who have killed the killers,
and with the *shanda*
the repeated *shanda*
and the ashes of memory astonished
that suddenly they themselves
are sitting *shivah* in the wind
blowing through everything,

unbutton your blood
down to your naked soul,
bend over, drop to your knees.

O tongue of oil between the violated
thighs of Iraq, whose open mouth
is Israel licking America's gun-butt
while the pornophony
of Palestine gangbanged by all three
sounds through the wall the gyzym
and saliva cries in twisted lascivia...

Yes, it's all clear now, all here now
are chosen: face down or eyes wide
shut in the *Razaya Yippalé*. Or wide
open as mouths around gun-barrels
shooting bullets into every orifice
in an orgy of lethal spunk.

O degenerate democracy,
your uprooted waves of grass are the
sea on which we cowed animals

walk and bend and chew. But
there's no rag for that 12-year period
at the heart of your thirst for blood
nor an end to the bulldozers of trash
you've totaled us with, we who are
smutten with your nothingness,
looking at each other through
asshole eyes.

So for those praying for the resistance,
arming themselves for the resistance,
gathering and committing their bodies
to the death in resistance,
we who've never dug into earth
to discover the roots
of the suicide that's ticking
in our ears every day,
we for whom peace is a pun
on a gun or a woman to screw
and who insist on values
the rest of the bleeding world
knows we've already
thrown away—

Exceptional America!
America the Exception
now demanding to be the rule
and the ruler as well
come down on mankind's open palm,

who beat off the Soviets
in a 36-year masturbation,

including the rape of Vietnam,
the snuffing of Guatemala,
the stacking of wads of dough
on the night-tables of Nicaragua,
El Salvador and Haiti, to secure
the brothelization of these days.

Empire? We're the underworld
of the world, led by a suited-up
gang of mobsters, a lucre-mad
Congress of cowards whose
callous indifference and outpourings
of bilge for the passage of laws of
extortion and trivia have insured
that it will take a man or woman
all of his or her life to become
a simple human being.

Empire indeed!
You giant indignity!
You humungous flop on the world's stage!

Only when, in just a few years, tough guy,
that "monster" (to use your already
war-mongering name for her), will have
overtaken you in every field of human
endeavor and humanity, and that people
both older and younger than you,
a billion strong, will say:
"We don't want you to make war
anymore anywhere on earth.
If you do we will stop you and your

weapons of mass destruction
without even a shot being fired.
We're the majority. You're an unruly child.
Go to the corner and learn your lesson"—

then, America, finally you'll be free.

THE HOUSE OF THE SETTING SUN

"Become a rag again and the poorest may wave you"
Pier Paolo Pasolini: To the Red Flag

I put my mouth to your misery, New Orleans,
inundated and soaking with death.
Here lies: war lies piled so high, this floating
prison of a cemetery cries out of rage
at the end of its breath. Here, in the last delta,
Desire lies on its side, is rolled, and rolled
over upon by its own government, and crushed.

Summertime is over and the livin' is dead,
and 'round midnight all hopes are looted.
No one will come clean of the Katrina
of New Orleans in this sinking
house of the setting sun.
Bodies so Black and so blue from loving
what wouldn't spit on their shoes if they
needed a shine. Let alone a dime. Or water.

America, you were always scorched earth
in our mouths, always a baptism of crap,
always a rain of disaster streaming
down the panes of our broken eyes.
Now our rags are the most torn,
our jazz the most blue, our poor the poorest
that can be worn in the soul's thrift-shop.
Now that all is lost and there's only nothing
to lose… "Long live the courage
and the sorrow and the innocence of the poor!"
The real flag's in tatters. Begin to wave it.

CAFFÉ TRIESTE

This central public place of my life for 34 years,
give or take journeys to Europe and Venezuela,
is where I've written hundreds of poems,
translated hundreds more from many languages,
where I wrote my first poems in Russian.

More than a café making terrific double espressos
it's a cultural center in the heart of old town San
Francisco that still shows a neon and glitzy world
what deep old brew really means. How so many
continue to meet here, fall in love, be the daily
chronicle and times to each other and where,
for 26 years, this just about oldest newsboy in town
has been selling the *People's Tribune* and *Rally Comrades*,
table after table, and don't forget, in the '80s, in the same
manner, *Compages*, that revolutionary international
magazine of translations of poetry from all over the world.

I don't forget Anna Magnani *la seconda*, beloved Yolanda,
now in Monfalcone, Italy but ever remembered as muse and
momma to a whole generation here. And Yolanda's Francesco,
and Leopoldo Fiorenzato, sensitive and tragic, and Taura and
Walker—workers through the years, gone elsewhere, to heaven
or Mexico, and yet here's Paul and Rabba and Hakim with his
newborn Adam, and roast-master Paul and Nathan and Sean
and Ernie and Ida—she who makes sure the people get their dose
of Italian poetry bilingually, along with the other languages
flying around, i.e., French, Algerian and Arabic—workers
close to the heart and the joys and the sorrows of this corner.

And let's not forget drop-ins like Allen Ginsberg a couple times
a year. And the local radiances like Lawrence Ferlinghetti, Bobby
Kaufman, Neeli Cherkovski, the poems flying amid the jukebox
music, the olding Beats and the Baby Beats and the commies,
the surrealists, the anarchists, the socialists, the jazzmen, the ultra
screwballs, the walk-in weirdoes, the beautiful women begun and
developed here, and the tots, those fooblezeegs, always so welcome
and alive at this street-level (not the United States of a dead mall but
the other America), of embodied old wood and deep flavor, with an
extended Italian family whose hands come out of their mouths
as well as arias and popular songs, and who know how, even with
the remembered loss of their and our prince of the human voice,
continuare, *continuare*, above all, singing because, with this room—
in its every corner, and along the outside tables as well—there's song.
Rilke was correct: *Gesang ist Dasein*—Song is Existence. That's
the real logos of this place; for wherever you travel, whether
to other states or foreign places, whether on the Vino Express
or the Shmoogadoo Limited, with the Caffé Trieste you'll always
have a direction home.

THE WAR DRUGS ON

The war drugs on, die after die.
Soldyeahs and chopped suichives mock
an ignomanyus fear of socult exisdunce
and Jams Juice tearns over
in his tome.

Tears over Bogdud as well,
and Feelootya is dust and smothereened
and all I rock is a mass sad, a djinnstone
of peer warking peoples and fearmas
without heaven a dutt of a dot

of utripia or a teatle of a tokapot.
Let's imputsch that warboyl
into the paypull's crapper! Let's biled
that ganghostar a jail rumi enoaf
for all his toxass bush-shit.

And peeyul the plague! And watch
him and his junta of assashenanalists
god down the stinking hole
they were shat up from
tobegunwad.

JACK KEROUAC: A MEDITATION

When I was
student young
one day the
Kerouac way

suddenly was
felt far and near
like an eruption
of the American

moment I'd only
been hanging around
or talking about
or studying about

but not living
in the sense of
being inside its
being inside me,

and from that time
forward I was
the word for my
self within:

My ear-drums
could sound.
The tympany
of my tongue

could mystify
with holy galores,
and the motion
of my breath

upon the waters
of the streets
where I'd wept
and hallelujahed

would become
the adventure of
the life I'd give
my life for:

Poetry! That's
Jack Kerouac's path
in verse and jazz
prosody: Poetry!

WALLACE BERMAN

There's movies, yes, the movies,
but at heart is the ear
to the radio in the car
of Cocteau in *Orphée*
making poetry.

There's music, yes. Hip before
even the hop, Bemsha's deeyop;
there's a Yod, which means
a hand,
which contains ten Yods

like in a quintet with Bird,
Miles, Trane, Monk and
Roach. And in that hand,
which is what
it holds:

a can of beer becomes
an AM-FM transistor
radio with a video
screen, all put together
to be lifted

to the eyes and tasted,
collage after collage,
formally eloquent or
laced with a hard core,
trendaciously sensual,

himself withdrawing as
he reveals, low-profiling
as he faces full on. And
since style without
content is death,

leaving a tracery of
holy doubletalk, like,
"Where the stattafore
and the frammis
part company…"

he did,
only to
never.

BOB KAUFMAN

I take the Fifth
Stoly World
Symphony
with no chaser

and see, through all
the Walls fallen down,
the break-up of the Union
and all the war-norms

and crass-consciousness
of these last 20 years,
Bob Kaufman
still wrapped in rainbows,

both arms upward,
both palms outward
and on his lips
the montage that began

at Scott Joplin's fingertips
with WB, Dylan, Allen, Joe,
Jack, Hart, John and Federico.
Who would die

for poetry. And did.
And this one's just one
of his many acolytes,
disciples, comrades

in the chorus of snot
that lashes capitalism's
monsters and spikes their
wine with lethal pot.

PAUL ROBESON

He who was stoned. Not drugged. Stoned
by fascist-thug rocks as he sang
for the People in Peekskill

in a vicious attack that 58 years later
remains the unforgettable
shame of shames of American culture;

whose voice was the ground where
all colors of the rainbow warmed themselves
on the black fire of his affirmations;

who entered our pores, who never separated
a forward pass, a Shakespearean soliloquy
or a workers' song from the revolutionary

transformation of all the world's peoples;
who IS the Old Man River flowing
into countless other voices

singing, when I open my mouth, singing
when you open yours, singing the dream
he rendered palpable, and vast, and deep.

HOMAGE TO KEN WAINIO

He always wrote with
that confidence in the inventions
of the imagination
that defines surrealism's
crossing the boards of our time
with wake-up calls
to Death to
  "Get outta bed!
   You gotta write a poem!"

So when he writes about looking
"through a pinprick in God's condom
to infinite worlds of the dictionary"
he's in his element:
Words, definitions. He managed
to look up everything.
"Even my skirt," said Kristen.
"Even my bibliography," said I.
So when we met, at that corner

table of Vesuvio's by the window,
and for some reason or other
I had taken off all my clothes,
Kenny, who knew a hairy story or two
about nudity, exclaimed:
The alchemists say the secret
of 86
is the Cherokee syllabary
and your Sequoyah's number's up.

Next thing I know it's 10 years later.
I'm rounding a corner when who's
in the driver's seat of a cab but Wainio.
"I'm a working stiff," he sing-songs,
"Bim-bam, bim-biff, you common nest."
And off he guns, to pick up the speed
of light in front of the Pagoda
moviehouse by the park. Which is dark
now. Now no more. O those many

zany days with ever young Wainio,
with his third eye spang in the middle
of his naked cranium: looking up,
always looking up.

NEVER AGAIN

They were gassed, burned by the millions
simply because they existed.
Those who survived said: Never Again!
They were asked to come to Hanoi
and continue the socialist revolution.
They responded: Never Again!

We will never again trust any government.
We will make our home in Palestine,
defeat the Arabs there, scatter them or
let them live as ragged shadows
in the camps of our occupation.
We will live in and on the capital of America,

as Israel, by name, as the Jewish nation,
and never again be holocausted for
the crime of simply being.
But even as Israel grew and prospered,
those whom it displaced and arrested
were whispering: Never Again!

Poor and landless, they built their resistance
and fought and lost again and again
to Zionism's army of American weapons.
The language of socialism, of the friendship
and harmony of peoples of different cultures
died of attrition in the Middle East, from

money. Deals. Dunny meals. Doomy mules.
Dummy moles. Mummy doles. The Star

of David unfurled over the land,
but the real Davids were in the streets
throwing stones at the Goliath.
O philistine irony and reversal of the Hebrew.

They who are the poorest and stateless,
who've turned their hatred of submission
to slavery into martyr brigades of suicided
human weapons, and called their brethren
to join their attack upon the ferocious colony
of the United States of Exploitation;

they, the poorest and homeless, in whom
the only solution still breathes, the only
solution that isn't genocide or fratricide
or a final solution itself, where hand-clasps
and words can still open the gates to the
language of the future socialism of New

Israel and New Palestine,
—where Never Again!
will be the united cry
of both, aimed
at the land of the fraud
and the home of the greed.

POETS ELEVEN POEM

Between the page with the heart
and the mind wrestling upon it,

and the ear which later will receive
those limbs of light as perfect harmony,

there's a stillness whose volume speaks
worlds of words defiant of measure,

treasures of the unsayable, secrets
of the ever-beginning enchantment

and the never-ending gathering
at the lips of the kiss of the poem.

THE NEWS

The homeless night
is descending
in us all.

Careless promises
come to a stand-still
wall.

Hopes become holes
in the daily, picked
pockets.

We speak and are
overheard by
someone paid

to rat in the Year
of the Dog.
The corpse-orate

world opens its dead
mouth. Out comes
all it knows:

Profits! Profits!
Jimmy dies beside
a dumpster,

Cynthia's living
inside one.
Five schools shut their

doors on kids, as Exxon
announces 36 billion
in Profits! Profits!

Mr. Mayor and Supes,
the people need you
to govern the corpse,

to insist it no longer
stink up the town
but must cough up,

keep coughing up
till it comes back
to human life.

In this homeless night
where even carpal
fingers darken with

job-loss fear, the war
and the lies and the
obscene machines of

Profits, our patience
is running out
into streets shouting:

Up to here! Up to here!
"We have been nothing,
we shall be all."

(Continue on next page,
with next demand, in
next action. Continue…)

THIS HOUSE OF HUNGER

For the American kids who
go to sleep each night without supper

This house of hunger has
millions of kids in it.
Breakfast and lunch is
all they're worth.

Fat Exxon and Bechtel
have billions of bux in them.
What pretty profits to set
before King Death!

Banks stink with the stench
of unmitigated greed.
Ms., Mr. and Mrs. Indifference
included in their digital speed,

while those kids lie abed
each night without even
a cup of bouillon in their
trembling hands.

O go kill the children in other
lands, America, you shootiful,
and cover for the murders
you plant in your own backyard.

Keep insisting you're democracy,
but in the starving darkness
those sad, lost eyes
know the truth of your icy lie:

that you've sold all the marbles,
in their little sacks
to the bullies who applaud because
they won't give them back,

and you've stolen the bread
that cried for their mouths
and turned it into dirty dough,
and that's why, when finally

they manage to fall asleep, their
dreams call you The Haunted House,
put a spell of the Sun on you
to burn you down,

so that greedy spirits flee,
and fields grow rapidly
good things for hungry
little bellies to eat.

THE DEPORTATION BLUES

I went to many countries
throughout the Americas
and told the people there
what we wanted to do.

"We want to deport Bush
and his top henchmen!"
But every one of those lands
absolutely refused.

"We're not a garbage dump,"
they said, "Nor a gangster refuge.
Those guys and that Rice have
War & Death in their eyes

and they'll stink up our streets
so that even our dogs will wonder
what kind of turds have come down,
what sort of new dog-flu?

Listen," they continued, "that gang
has made it so that when our poor
are forced to flee the poverty
their corporations have cooked up,

we face death at their borders
or, if caught, deportation.
Instead of being welcomed into
their nation, given passports,

allowed to come and go like
any ordinary *hermana y hermano*,
we have to live and work like
criminals for slave-labor wages

with deportation over our heads.
And they're always tightening
the screws, even on these Blues,
so until they come to their

immigration senses, and be like
the words on the Statue of Liberty,
you can take that *junta* of rotten herrings
and dump it in the cold dark sea."

VENEZIA

I was enraged
at your body,
Venezia,
when I first saw
your bauble shops,
chic chicanery
that cried out,
"Buy my glittering
dribble of an
awful orgasm
spurted onto
my Rialto
Bridge thighs!"

Slowly I found
your side-streets
where you practice
a strolling stillness
without any
engine sounds,
under a sky turning
into the color of
spriz con aperol
and then into
a turner-burnished
magnificence of
twilight where

a hidden flame
of affectionate

heart accompanies
your every move,
and there's no
doubt about it,
you're more
adorable without
a car wrapped
around you, where
you can be what
you are:
walking water

that gently laps,
and that's why
I've come to you
this midnight
and lain down
in your black body
with its soft
red plush, and
pulled the startling
blue cover over
our rocking under
a cheek of moon
blushing through the mist.

DJUNA

That she'd lived and written on Ward Ave.,
three blocks from the street
in The Bronx I grew up on
13 years before I even was born...

"And just what are you getting at,"
says Djuna,
"bones?"

And that an alphabet of years later I'd be
dissertating on her masterpiece
of poetic prose, and writing
a bestiary of poems.

"And what might that mean
to a blue tureen," says Djuna,
"scones?"

47 years later she's long since ash.
The world's become unmitigated cash.
A woman gazing into the face
of her cell-phone.

"'I gave my love a cherry,'"
says Djuna, "and lived on
raging puns."

So endure, endure these bitter
hops of hips, and hopheads
in the banal galore of empty
claps.

Nightwood still holds up,
after all these years, like
a garterbelt's thunder-snap.

THE KICK ARCANE

1.

The sorrow these many months
isn't because Laureate celebrity's
put eyes all over my body,

as if I were in the U.S. again, not
the other America. It comes from the
footprint of a kick-stab in my back

got riding a bus to a reading with
some really destitute brothers and
sisters in a 16th St. office space.

I'm sitting in the rear of the bus reading
a translation of the *Book of the
Concealed Mystery*, when my eyes

are lifted from the pages by the high
voice of a young Black woman standing
and talking on her cell-phone.

Her voice decibels above the seated,
dog-tired Latino, Black and White workers
en route home, and when I rise to exit

accidentally grazing her sleeve as I pass
with an "Excuse me," she pushes me, shouts,
"Don't touch me!" with a hatred and ferocity

makes me turn, shout in return "And what
the hell dya think you just did to me?!"
And for an instant face a pair of eyes coiled

in cold rage and denial all at once and set
to spring—when, around my shoulders,
I feel a pair of gentle but insistent arms

and half-turning hear from a young Black
man with an almost consoling smile: "You
don' wanna go there…Here's your stop."

He leads me to the stairwell. But no sooner
do I begun descending when I feel myself
hurtled down by a kick to my back, falling

and landing awobble on my feet as the door
closes with a snicker and the bus pulls away
from my amazement. "What'd they do?"

a Latina asks in startled urgency on the sidewalk,
and her words make me realize I'm 72
for the first time in my life.

2.

One could I suppose Chaplin it away, how for
no reason suddenly one is bopped, clobbered
with club or cane, kicked in the ass

for a slapstick laugh in the silence of the Silents.
But it just happens humiliation sounds one's
very depths; just happens, a wound

knows no death of time, and not so random is
the karma of lungs breathing archaically and
post-modernly together; just happens I didn't know

the volatility of the hatred of man-touch or white
man-touch and so could only think: junkie, or dyke.
But if the prophecy be true, that "Negritude will be

reason…" and reason must find its violence in order
to be (for violence at bottom is the memory of a
horror carried by the soul of blood to the blood of sex),

she, a violence of resistance, is also a violence for,
as if she'd said, "Awe of me? Why not take awe
of me, and shove it up your ass, 'cause it can just about

fit where the shit you are lives, 'cause I'm inside you now,
in violation of you, immaculately, you American—filthy
crumb of a loaf of no people. I'm here and everywhere,

and you no matter how old always will be the snot-nose
with adolescent shame spread over your brains from
a rumble-down cellar of gangbang wooden zips,

where the real thing went down on eight for a tenner each,
then ran in torn shreds of a dead dawn to bring hot rolls
and milk to two kids in a dump near Palou.

3.

Chalk it up like the gutters and walls of our breath
or the blue-tipped stick stood up between jilted thighs,
singing: The day is night and the night knows only

the inside of this long lonesome bread of blues. Don't
climb to the top of the old coal-bin, hear? You can
fall in and we'll never again find you.

So many tongues, at the midnight taint, paint the world
where the sunshine ain't. Go back? To what beginning?
A serial suck? A kick in the butt? O desolate

animal of leather pelt in this hell's night wood, stay
clopen. Be full of distress—you can't pull the race
card out of your hat. She the mother of memories,

the *ur-schrei* of the originary No. And you can't pull
the race card out of the bitch's bra neither. And if she
push you and kick you, curse and spit 'cause you who

touched her raped her mother and grandmother, and
mine! You can't do shit. We the thunder that never
stops shaking roofs, we born to hate hate learned hate

was white, and then that white didn't mean shit or shinola,
it just mean meaninglessness, no reason, fed intravenously
and vaingloriously feeding the rebus where I B I and U B U

and nothing will ever B between but tragic race disgrace
'cause U and I R on Q to B slaves Black and White, that's Y.
The consumer tree's grown long long limbs. There's money

in rage and murder. Bloody blood-talk. War dough. War duh.
Everyone riding humpback in their own doggy hegemony.
B & W, you naughted states of a putrid klan of worms,

insane and gravely dangerous, put your "sincere ignorance
and conscientious stupidity" away. Come together from
under the skin where soul is blood and needs the sea,

and ride the wave and the furl of Class, the only war that's
peace, to the end of civic death and money's tyranny,
and be what Revolution means as the Way that has to be!

MUMIA

This will get to you,
Mumia, I know,
one way or another,
you know
you have a vast
number of people
who know
you're only guilty
of innocence
and yours will be
victorious—that
we all of us know.

Not simply here but
in France, Spain,
Germany, Italy
as well as Haiti,
Cuba, Palestine,
Israel, Africa
—in fact everywhere
books are translated
or the Web can reach
and your name and
your courageous writings
and your daily travail

are known, your victory
will be the priceless up-
lifting of human spirit.
For we're all sick of

Death and its wars
for oil and profits,
the murdering of
innocents, the suiciding,
the genociding, the
therefore Dafur,
the cost of holocaust.

Mumia, I know you
know there's only one
reason you've not only
stood by your words
but lived to enunciate
their truths from inside
the cell of death where
they've thrown you:
not to save your neck
but to mend the broken
one of the world; not to
simply express yourself

but to project from the
loneliest pit the enthralling
light of the need for
revolutionary transformation.
You are the Nazim Hikmet
of the American grain,
that Turkish poet who
spent 26 years in prison
and who, in a poem of

only two pages, entitled,
"Ever Since They Threw
Me In Here," revealed

how no amount of bars
or shackles can chain
the revolutionary impulse
in the human heart.
Like you, poet. Yes, you,
Mumia Abu-Jamal, poet
of our daily struggles,
writing from hell itself,
(and make no mistake,
brothers and sisters,
anyone born from that
radiant and incendiary

Manifesto that neither the
forced amnesia or the
alzheimerization of
societies can make
one forget, knows there's
no difference between
poetry and prose); for you,
Mumia, have turned the fires
of hell into flames of the
highest honor. A man
most free must from
his physical

enslavement
be freed
to greet the
widespread
wide-open
arms of
a world
that he
—simply put—
has taught
so much
liberty.

FIDEL CASTRO

The president of the other America has fallen ill
and it's his birthday. We wish him Happy
Birthday and a speedy recovery.

By the other America, we don't simply mean
his brothers and sisters in Venezuela, Bolivia,
Chile, Peru, Brazil, Haiti, and the like.

We mean also the 37 million people living destitute
and in misery in these disunited States, of whom
million of kids go to bed hungry every night,

while a murder machine waves the false flag of security
and makes war on the poor of the world.
What is more insecure than the empty belly of a child?

The president of the other America knows that there is
a poverty that is the wealth of the world. *Viva* the poverty
of Cuba that makes even the comrade on the cross applaud.

Viva the dignity of Cuba, whose island arms stretch
all the way to the equality of love that is Africa.
There is a man who has understood that life is worth

nothing if it is not free, and freedom nothing if it is not
consciousness of necessity—principled, palpable and priceless.
That is Fidel. That is *fidelidad*. Be well, comandante. *Feliz cumpleaños.*

CUBA WISER

In a poem I wrote earlier this year
I described capitalism as a pack
of "rabid attack dogs destroying
each other over hunks of money."
We see the truth of that image everyday
in Iraq, Afghanistan, Israel and Lebanon:
Dead children's limbs in the jaws of
those mongrels of greed, wails of women
drowned in the barkness that's biting
their sorrow to shreds. Cuba-wise,
we know there's only one process to peace:
the palpable voyage of human discourse
along paths of the hoped-for socialism.
From the belly of the beast of beasts,
in a time of a contagion of ravines
and a pestilence of superfluous things,
I invoke you, necessary island, principled main
for all revolutionary fighters,
helmsman through this cybernetic sea aflame,
with your visionary eyes. Cuba wiser.

THE SUSIE ARCANE

In Memory of Susan Birkeland

I.

Strangely as if the lid
of her own coffin were
closing over her

just when people are
reading her words,
she's quietly resting

cherishing thoughts of
the thoughtlessness
she's slipping into,

of looking the inner one
in the eye and finally
being zero.

So no more boats to
go down to the piers for.
Yet, still wanting, in the

waning, mistily she strains
upward: the other side,
all who've died, seems

alive and kicking. She
wants to be there.
She's dying to be.

She's waiting for him
to come over her, to
take her out.

Who never fails. Him.
Above all. Who'll carry
her away to she.

Nothing more. No doubt.
She has next to nothing
to do but check out.

II.

Say there are places in
San Francisco sparkling
with the serious *joie*

de vivre of her poems
read from that core of
crisp bright soul,

that the North Beach
corner where she sang
with friends and wine

and shmoogadoo really
feels posthumous. "Those
were the days…Ladadadadada."

Her eyes now ready, her
breast now ready, her hips
and thighs and modesty as well.

Darn, she just would like
to know when she'll
arrive at that language

she's been written by. Hands
are in hers, holding on. Do
you read me in the darkness

when the light is on? O yes,
yes, open to ten thousand
things. The humming

of butter melting on his
body, for one. But all's
overing, ovary just

can't be. Yes, yes, it can.
Where it isn't. Here. In
memory of the morning sun.

III.

Death being what it is,
you know, and that's
why she is too.

Susie, dear Susie
with your brave spiral
of rage and tenderness,

projective and scored.
Among so many street
poets how brightly you

shone, enthusing, a
blushing leaf of grass
who could burn at

Abu Ghraib, and chide
a celebrity brother for
forgetting his and your

hometown of Hibbing.
O Death, you rat, you bit
into Susie just when she

was coming to full poem
prime. Here's your cheese,
Death. Be snapped to death

for taking Susie. Poetry's
so sad about not being
able to be written by her,

it's gone to a corner and
won't come out until
she speaks again.

And of course, being poetry
now, she does.
She exclaims:

"I jump with glee!
I make voluminous tea
for all the entities

that are my friends in the
morning. Have some. It's me.
Have some of me.

It's good.
It's good and warm
in the morning."

SNAPPY-GO-ROUND
For Ira Nowinsky

I remember a night of wild incantations.
naked strophes. Kettle-drumming youth.
And you there, snappy-go-round,
shooting us full of ourselves,
negatives and positives at the end
of that war that defined us as a generation
of dissenters.

You understood we all were there in
Caffé Trieste society or the bars down
the road, to get away from the United States,
that our poems were the passports out,
that any moment along Grant Street
anyone of us could run into a Third Eye,
lift its lid and see

the Eye was really you. And you'd go on,
go downtown catching the depth, sadness
and dignity in old souls in old hotels.
And how apt the opera, for Song is Existence
and a poem its genesis. I remember one
that's never stopped kissing you, because
you've shown darkness what it means to be light.

FOR THE NEW YEAR 2007

O happy beginning, baby-step year, unfold
as a love affair knowing no past, going breathlessly
forward toward where you came from and are:
—all future, with caresses of innocence.

I don't want last year's desert of snow,
bodies face-down dead of war on my own,
the lies and trivia that framed us up,
hopes rapidly rotted, dignities impaled,
drinks that drank us to bottomless pits,
tokes that turned off hearing anything
        but The Ego Rag.

O show us the way to be human, after all,
to listen as beginners to beginning's call
to open our minds so our hearts shine clear,
and all will be an intimate whisper

wanting to make love to you all year strong,
wanting to share peace with you under the banner
of Beginning, so that there's no end of it
for anyone anywhere.

ALL THAT'S LEFT

All that's Left
    in the world
—whether in Cuba, Venezuela, Bolivia
as well as in China, Japan, the United States,
Europe, the Middle East, Africa—
all of them cannot,
   despite their resistance,
   despite their refusal,
stop this march of death
because they,
as well as all that's Right
in the world,
   despite their refusal,
   despite their resistance,
already are counted among those
   in this last parade.
Communists and progressives,
nazis, fascists and reactionaries,
zionists and anarchists of every stripe—
none are excluded, none can evade the march.

This one's not coming
with hammer and sickles or swastikas
or flags of any land.

This one's the march
all wars surrender to.

But when?! comes the unanimous cry.
When will it really happen?
If death is peace,
when can I truly die?

You will never know, and yet you do,
because you may already have,
and this life is your way
of paying homage to the power
that loves you enough
to have taken your life away
and left you with the taste
of immortality on your lips.

Nothing mystical: no Christ,
Allah, Jahweh or Buddha in the wings.
Even lying on your back you're marching.

This is not a cynical or pessimist
or nihilist poem. Join death
to your life and you will live
as if there were no drum to march to.

There is no march at all.

You're there. All will be well for all.

THE WAYS OF LOVE ARCANE

"Only in its being gone does it exist,"
I whispered in the candle-lit dark.

Your response was the art of loving
which is a part of what I meant.

And it was a masterpiece you wrote
with your tongue.

***

But is Love gone? That love, yes, has.
But there's no end of loving here

or wherever you are, or even where
nowhere is.

It's not a fool or a rule, it doesn't mistake
the image for its intended effect,

like eating vodka. It includes the image
and the eaten vodka because it began

both of them in the first place by simply
being Being. A man knows no other

word for it except perhaps to write a poem,
and he does that even fitting a screw

into a wall, or drinking a cold glass of beer,
or hooraying at a sports event,

or wearing his woman's brassiere, that's how
everything it is.

***

You cling to my mouth and I to yours
because the meaning of us is our voices.

I fell for yours before I knew what the rest
of your body can do.

The japasutram of your mouth already was
preparing this mat of soft straw

on which we're set in an erotic iconography
many turn the pages of and see

us delighting in making love to the sound
of their eyes.

That is the commune of voices our own
have striven to bring to a world

disappearing into voicelessness. Your lips
obsess me, above and below.

How they adore being the two fingers of a
swooning sigh. And with my body

half-turned, legs spread high apart, how
your tongue at my taint and your ream

ecstasizes me to bury my own in the depths
of that rose that never is seen except,

fold by lobe and petal by petal, by a braille
my tongue alone reads, opening the sun

in the darkness to the slow explosions of
blinding inner sight.

***

This primitive of me is natural. Mind is not.
Hey, animal, show me your instincts.

They won't scare me, even unto death.
Mind does.

I'd like to go to sleep with utter mindlessness.
I'd stroke your nipples and now

that the rain's falling go between the drops
with my want of all your tit.

This is a form of mindless reason grounded
in the reign of body. Nothing would be

a shiver in the wind if we didn't give it shape.
Mind does that, but from the body mind is in.

So admit: Body's all. Mind should be that, but
only when it's lost does it become true body.

Your body came to me through a bodily
gesture that was mine on yours. It began

the end of your mind though you fight like
the dickens to keep it.

Our love is mindless, that is we truly care
and don't just stare at it.

***

And if I whisper, if I but move in the minutest
way, I'm so afraid of losing you, I would die

of being unable to wake beside your shape;
and so I freeze in my heat and let you rummage

through my body, pat, softly slap my ass and play
under my bra (which I always wear because

my breasts are afraid of your hands except when
I'm sitting straight up on you and you whisper

how extraordinarily ripe and voluptuous they are
for one as old as I am).

***

You tell me I make loud animal sounds in my sleep.
I am an animal. I'm a buffalo-unicorn. A bare bear.

I eat the depths of meat and bite its lips. I swell
with smitten and yoga on the belly of your sex.

I am sated with emptiness as in a sutra. Let's face
it: the best of us is Buddhist, the vestigial

bone of the bone of shmoogadoo I smoked last
night, made love with you, slept ten hours

gloriously without any animal sounds, and so
can't sleep tonight without writing this poem.

Want another? I'll give you another anytime.
I'm a man. Past a point I'm afraid of nothing.

O for those *Floating Bear* days when we wrote
hugs and published our syllables along with our feet.

***

Listen, this is the sound of my sleepless breathing.
I know nothing but this slavery.

I never intended it, it fell into my arms, a silent
abundance. I couldn't keep it away from

the center of my essence, and now it's too late,
I'm gone to the dogs with you. Everything is

nothing until you wipe my ass with your kisses
and I go forward back to originary light.

***

I'm going to alight on your sleeping eyelid and close
my wings there. And sleep with you as if there were

no need anymore to waken. And when the sun rises,
it will be inside you, and I'll see everything.

VIRGINIA TECH

The "loner" is me,
the one who stopped listening,
the one with the hidden fuse,
with the fist of blind clench,
with the hole in his heart,
with the cool guns,
the one who blasts away,
who kills because, just because,
who kills at will and, because
there's nothing left but the dead,
kills himself,
suicided on top of all he's killed,
and now you know what a market
in old Baghdad feels like
with its victims "in the wrong place
at the wrong time,"
and why your mourning is going
in one ear of the deaf tomorrow
and out the deafening other.

With the exception of the first seven poems, which were composed in the months just prior to my having been selected as the Poet Laureate for the City of San Francisco in January 2006, all the poems in this volume were written during the Laureate period. Some of them have appeared in: *The People's Tribune*, *Left Curve*, *Street Sheet*, *Poesy*, *Parthenon West Review*, *CAC* (Catalog), and *Il Manifesto* (in Italian translation). My thanks to the Editors.

—Jack Hirschman